WILFRITH ELSTOB VC DSO MC
The Manchester Regiment

"Here we fight. Here we die"

Robert Bonner

Published in 1998
by
Fleur de Lys Publishing, Knutsford, Cheshire.

Copyright © Text 1998 by Robert A Bonner.
Copyright © Illustration 1998 by the Trustees of The Manchester Regiment Collection.

All rights reserved.
Without limiting the rights under copyright
reserved above, no part of this publication may be
reproduced, stored in or introduced into a retrieval system,
or transmitted, in any form or by any means (electronic, mechanical,
photocopying, recording or otherwise), without the prior
written permission of both the copyright owner and
the above publisher of this book.

A catalogue entry for this book is available from the British Library.

ISBN 1-873907-08.7

CONTENTS

FOREWORD
VII

ILLUSTRATIONS
IX

PREFACE
X

VICTORIA CROSS CITATION
XII

1888-1915
1

1916
5

1917
6

1918
13

MANCHESTER HILL
14

EPILOGUE
18

1923
22

1993
24

1994
25

1996
26

INDEX
29

BIBLIOGRAPHY
33

Dedication

To the everlasting memory of the young men
of Manchester and district who formed the
1st Pals Battalion, later renamed the
16th Battalion of The Manchester Regiment.

FOREWORD

The King's or 8th Regiment of Foot was formed in 1683 and in 1758 its 2nd Battalion was renamed as the 63rd Regiment of Foot. In 1881 the 63rd amalgamated with the 96th Regiment to form The Manchester Regiment and the 8th Regiment was retitled The King's (Liverpool) Regiment. In 1958 these two regiments amalgamated to form The King's Regiment – a reunion after 200 years.

This volume is the first in a series describing the lives of the twenty three soldiers of The King's (Liverpool) Regiment and The Manchester Regiment who have been awarded the Victoria Cross.

I am grateful in so many ways for the support and interest of my good friends in The Regiment but particularly Lieutenant Colonel Rex King-Clark MBE MC, Major Robert Clutterbuck and Crispin Worthington who also saw active service as a National Service officer with The Manchesters during the Malayan Emergency.

I am reminded by my friend Michael Stedman that the 16th Manchesters were involved in all the significant 'opening days' of the major set piece battles of the Western Front.

Knutsford
May 1998   RAB

ACKNOWLEDGEMENTS

I am grateful to the Worthington family for permission to print the extracts from the correspondence between Hubert Worthington and Wilfrith Elstob; to Tony Nash for giving permission to publish the letter from Wilfrith Elstob to his Father which appears in 'The Diary of an Unprofessional Soldier'.

ILLUSTRATIONS

WILFRITH ELSTOB
XI

THE ELSTOB MEDALS
XIII

SIDDINGTON CHURCH
XIV

HEATON PARK
2 & 3

SKETCH BY HUBERT WORTHINGTON
4

OFFICERS GROUP, RENINGHELST
13

MANCHESTER HILL DEFENCES
15

MEMORIAL SERVICE PROGRAMME
18

LETTERS FROM CANON ELSTOB
19/20

MANCHESTER UNIVERSITY WAR MEMORIAL
21

SIDDINGTON CHURCH PLAQUE
22

SIDDINGTON CHURCH MEMORIAL WINDOW
23

MONTAUBAN 1994
25

FRANCILLY SELENCY
26 & 27

THE RYLEYS SCHOOL MEMORIAL
POZIERES MILITARY CEMETERY
28

PREFACE

"It is the fact that some men possess an inbred superiority which gives them a dominating influence over their contemporaries, and marks them out unmistakably for leadership. This phenomenon is as certain as it is mysterious. It is apparent in every association of human beings in every variety of circumstances and on every plane of culture. In a school among the boys, in a college among the students, in a factory, shipyard or mine among the workmen, as certainly as in the Church and in the Nation, there are those who, with an assured and unquestioned title, take the leading place, and shape the general conduct,"

The Lord Bishop of Durham, *Walker Trust Lecture on Leadership* 1934, before the University of St. Andrews.

XII

LIEUTENANT COLONEL WILFRITH ELSTOB
16th BATTALION THE MANCHESTER REGIMENT
21st March 1918 at Manchester Redoubt near St Quentin, France

During the preliminary bombardment he encouraged his men in the posts in the Redoubt by frequent visits. When repeated attacks developed he controlled the defence at the points threatened, giving personal support with revolver, rifle and bombs.

Single-handed he repulsed one bombing assault, driving back the enemy and inflicting severe casualties. Later, when ammunition was required, he made several journeys under severe fire in order to replenish the supply. Throughout the day, although twice wounded he showed the most fearless disregard of his own safety and by his encouragement and noble example inspired his command to the fullest degree.

The Manchester Redoubt was surrounded in the first wave of the enemy attack, but by means of the buried cable, Lieutenant Colonel Elstob was able to assure his Brigade Commander "that the Manchester Regiment will defend Manchester Hill to the last".

Some time later the post was overcome by vastly superior forces and this very gallant officer was killed in the final assault. He maintained to the end the duty which he impressed on his men, namely, "Here we fight and here we die".

Siddington Church, Cheshire.

WILFRITH ELSTOB VC DSO MC
1888 - 1918

Wilfrith Elstob was born on 8th September 1888 in Chichester, Sussex, where his father, John George Elstob, was a priest-vicar of the Cathedral. His mother was Francis Alice Chamberlain. Six weeks later the family moved to Cheshire where his father had been appointed Vicar of Capesthorne with Siddington, a rural parish near Chelford.

The young Elstob went to the nearby Ryleys Preparatory School in Alderley Edge and from there in 1898 to Christ's Hospital, the famous Bluecoat School, then located in London. There he became a house monitor in Coleridge B and a hard-working forward in the rugby 1st XV. Then in 1905 to Manchester University, gaining his BA in 1909 and his teaching diploma in 1910. Wasting no time he then spent a year at the Lycee in Beauvais and another year studying at the Sorbonne in Paris. It was whilst he was at Beauvais that he wrote to a friend "Character depends upon the will".

Six foot one inch tall, he was a fine figure of a man. Sympathetic and dignified, with strong loyalty to his friends he was deeply religious in the best sense of that often misused description. To his friends he combined something of the ascetic with great physical strength of which he was almost unaware. A twenty mile walk with "Big Ben" or "Bindy" as he was known, could be a gruelling experience for his companions.

In 1912, after his year in Paris, he joined the Preparatory School of Merchiston Castle School in Edinburgh as senior French Master. It was at that time that a friend observed how he loved his chosen profession of schoolmaster with its immense potential for serving others and the opportunity of using his ability to inspire youth with the desire for higher achievements.

1914/1915

Following the outbreak of war in August 1914 Elstob enlisted on 11th September in the Public Schools Battalion. However on the night before setting off to Epsom to commence training he was offered and accepted a commission in the newly formed 1st Manchester Pals Battalion - later numbered 16th Battalion The Manchester Regiment - where he joined "A" Company as Second in Command to his lifelong friend Hubert Worthington[1] and was commissioned as 2nd Lieutenant on 30th October 1914.

The 16th Battalion had been raised in Manchester on 1st September 1914 and was the first of the nine Pals Battalions raised to The Manchester Regiment. This battalion was formed from volunteers who were clerks and warehousemen from Manchester's central commercial district. Employees from the large firms being placed into the same platoons where possible. Ex-Regular Army Non-Commissioned Officers were found to lick the raw material into shape. Young officers, such as Elstob, were selected from candidates for commissions and the senior officers were found from those with previous military experience.

On the 9th 'A' Company moved to Heaton Park on the outskirts of the city to establish a tented camp there. Heaton Park formed an excellent training ground and after six to seven weeks huts were built to replace the tents. Training proceeded at speed and seven months later on 31st March 1915 the 16th, with the rest of the Pals Battalions, paraded through Albert Square, Manchester where Lord Kitchener took the salute - 12,000 men in all.

1914. Heaton Park, Manchester.
The early days.

1915. Heaton Park, Manchester.

Number 4 Platoon, 'A' Company, 16th Manchesters. Captain Elstob is Company 2 i/c seated in the centre of the second row, behind drum. The Platoon Sergeant is J C Williams. Elsewhere in the photograph is Private S P Dawson, later to be awarded the Military Medal. After the war he joined the Territorial Army and rose to command the 8th (Ardwick) Battalion of The Manchesters, appointed Lord Mayor of Manchester in 1951 and Honorary Colonel of the 8th Battalion in 1956.

21st April 1915. Heaton Park, Manchester. The Pals Sports Day.

Brigade sports were held on 21st April at Heaton Park and formed a fitting occasion for a final leave taking from Manchester. 2nd Lieutenant Elstob captained an officers tug of war team. Huge crowds, estimated at 20,000, watched the events – the 16th Battalion winning the championship cup. Leaving Manchester on the 24th the battalion entrained for Grantham where training was continued until they moved to Larkhill Camp on Salisbury Plain for their final training.

5th January 1915. Following a march through the City, the Pals Battalions assembled for a band concert in the Free Trade Hall and an address by Brigadier General Westropp. Wilfrith Elstob is sitting in the second right hand row of steps, next to Hubert Worthington who is next to the aisle.

On 6th November 1915 the battalion moved to Folkestone, as part of 90th Brigade, and embarked for Boulogne. Elstob had been promoted acting Captain in May and was still second in command to Hubert Worthington in 'A' Company. Following a short spell of training in snow and ice at St. Ricquer the battalion moved off on the 17th to begin a long trek through many miles of France, arriving eventually for their baptism of fire on 7th December at the village of Hebuterne.

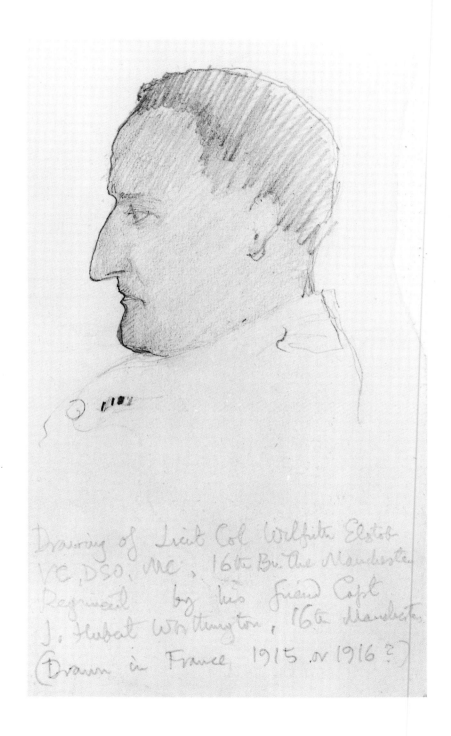

Drawing of Lieut Col Wilfrith Elstob
VC, DSO, MC, 16th Bn the Manchester
Regiment by his friend Capt.
J. Hubert Worthington, 16th Manchesters.
(Drawn in France, 1915 or 1916?)

1916

In March Elstob was given command of 'D' Company. Although engaged in unpleasant and dangerous duties in the trenches during the spring of 1916 the 16th experienced their first important action against the enemy with the great attack on the Somme of 1st July 1916. During the extensive fighting in and around the village of Montauban he was slightly wounded in the neck by a machine-gun bullet. One of his sergeants bandaged him with his handkerchief so that he could carry on. His great friend Hubert Worthington, commanding 'A' Company was severely wounded in lung, hand and thigh. Captain F Walker DCM[2], commanding 'B' Company, lost both his eyes and Captain Johnson[3] of 'C' Company was killed during the final counter attack. Lieutenant Allen[4] was killed whilst trying to rescue Lieutenant Kerry[5] who subsequently died from his wounds. For his leadership at Montauban Captain Elstob was later awarded the Military Cross.

This was the last time that the original 16th could be said to exist intact. The battalion which had fought at Montauban was still the battalion of Clerks and Warehousemen who had volunteered of their own free will at the beginning of the war and who were still led by their original leaders. But after that eventful 1st July only three hundred survived to fight again in the next battle. The remnants of the battalion withdrew to Happy Valley on the Bray/Albert road.

Eight days later on 9th July the battalion took part in operations around Trones Wood in support of the 17th and 18th Pals Battalions of The Manchesters and Elstob was wounded yet again. The 16th had lost 3 officers and 15 other ranks killed, 85 wounded and 85 missing. By this time the 16th Battalion had done splendidly at Montauban and Trones Wood but drafts of reinforcement were needed and came from 28 different units. On 10th July Elstob was appointed Second in Command of the battalion. Following the battle for Guillement on 30th July, in which the 16th lost 7 officers and 17 other ranks killed, 98 wounded and 97 missing, the battalion enjoyed a quiet period out of the front line throughout August

September 3rd found the battalion back in the front line until the 17th, after which they spent the rest of the month training and moving to various reserve locations. On 12th October 1916 the 16th moved into the front line near Le Barque to reinforce the devastated companies of the 17th and 18th Manchesters. This was accomplished by 10pm. During the following day they were heavily shelled and Lieutenant Colonel Knox[6], the Commanding Officer, decided to move his Headquarters to a safer position but was himself killed by a shell burst whilst making the move. That evening the 28 year old Major Elstob took over command of the battalion and was later appointed acting Lieutenant Colonel.

The following week was a most difficult one for everyone in the battalion as by this time the ground and trenches had been turned into a quagmire from the rain and constant artillery barrage. After a brief rest the 16th were back in the trenches on 29th October. Both November and December passed relatively quietly with a routine of 5 days in the trenches and 5 days in support or in reserve billets. The last tour of the front line of this sector began on the 30th December and on the 8th January 1917 the battalion moved to billets in Warlutz and on the 24th to Dainville near Arras.

In the diary which he kept at this time, Captain 'Beau' Nash[7] refers to an officer not returning to the battalion, presumably following leave, as Elstob had taken a dislike to him. This was based on the fact that during a relief in the trenches he had left a soldier behind who had been killed instead of bringing him out for burial. "In the 16th we made a point of never leaving a man behind us".

1917

Two months were now spent in supplying working parties to help a Canadian Pioneer Battalion in railway construction. Similar work occupied the battalion until mid-March when they were engaged in a period of semi-open warfare advancing some hundred yards or so every night. The battle of Arras began, in atrocious weather, on 9th April. The battalion was not brought into action until the following day when, at 2 pm, they were met with heavy machine-gun and rifle fire near St Martin. Then followed 24 hours of intensive fighting until relieved by the 18th Manchesters.

In a letter dated 15th April to his friend Hubert Worthington, Elstob wrote:

> "....it reached me last night, the day that we returned from the battle area.
>
> We have not been heavily engaged so that our casualties are few I am glad to say. The other two brigades lost heavily, but we were not thrown in, and we had nothing but outpost affrays in which the battalion did well and pleased the powers that be.
>
> My old platoon, number 'Eight' seized an important cross-roads, beat off a Boche counter-attack and took five prisoners so that they did jolly well, and I have just sent in the sergeant's name for a DCM which we all hope and believe that he will get. There was no officer with the platoon, Leech[8] was the Sergeant's name, you would not remember him, but the above will show he is a gallant fellow.
>
> "A" Company led into action by Hook[9] (Megson[10] behind) beat off a Boche counter-attack by rifle and rifle-grenade fire. It was most successful and the men were very pleased with themselves. The men were in splendid spirits.
>
> It is impossible to realise what "Destruction" means until one has seen the country laid waste by the Boche in his retreat. Every village is blown to bits; every cross-roads blown up; every bridge ditto - there is absolutely nothing except wreckage and desolation.
>
> I was very interested to hear about Claude[11], if I get half a chance I shall be over to see him."

On the afternoon of the 18th the battalion marched to a section of trenches in the Neuville-Vitasse area, arriving there in the early hours of the following morning. They later moved to forward positions in readiness for their coming offensive which had been planned on a 'leap frog' basis with the 16th supplying special bombing parties in addition to acting in close support.

90th Brigade began its attacks at 4.45 am on the 23rd against German positions at Cherisey, east of Heninel. 17th Manchesters were on the right, 2nd Royal Scots Fusiliers on the left with the 16th in immediate support. The advance was met by extremely heavy machine gun fire and a destructive artillery barrage. Elstob decided to carry out a personal reconnaissance and his report graphically describes the confusion and difficulties which faced the remnants of the assault battalions in their forward positions.

> "I went along the left of our old front line and down the trench going east from about N.30.a.7.2. Some 150 yards down this trench I found another trench leading off to the left and a few yards along that trench I found Lieutenant Wright of the 2nd RSF with their Coy HQ - He informed me that Colonel

McConaghy[12] and the Adjutant had gone forward and had not been seen since, though he had heard that both of them were wounded.

A number of men of RSF, 16th and 17th Manchester Rgt scattered about in isolated parties in shell holes. Enemy very active with snipers and MGs which it appeared had held attack up

Bde signals got a line up to this point (N.30.a.9.1 approx) and I communicated with the Brigade Major mentioning that the situation was very obscure but that I was endeavouring to clear it up and that a flank attack up the valley would probably clear the enemy out.

Received instructions to take charge and organise the attack.

Instructed Lt Wright to take charge of the 2nd RSF and any of their parties of men near lines and to organise a defensive position along the trench he was in, also to thin out the men and form them into groups under a NCO or a senior private.

Then went forward to try and discover where our front line actually had got to - on the way met Capt Hendrie of Stokes Mortar Battery and explained my intention of organising an attack up the valley, arranging for him to bring fire to bear on the left to occupy the attention of the enemy as soon as he saw party approaching up the valley. Capt Hendrie then went to reconnoitre the position for his guns.

I then went on towards the QUARRY and , leaving the trench, formed up some isolated parties of men in shell holes - It was necessary to crawl the whole time as ground was covered with M.G and rifle fire - I could not find any officers, so instructed each party that I came across to continue consolidating the shell holes that they were in and to hold on to them.

In the most forward shell hole that I reached I found one of our Sgts and 3 men. This Sgt informed me that the enemy were only about 25 yds away - He pointed out where he thought our left flank was (about N.30.b.4.4) and told me that at about 8.00am 60 Boche had attacked from a trench but had been driven off by Lewis Gun and Rifle fire. He said it was impossible to move from the shell holes without being shot.

I asked this Sgt whether he thought he was strong enough to hold the Boche on his immediate front and he replied, "Certainly sir, we've done it once and we can do it again."

I told him that I was going to organise a flank attack up the valley from the copse on the right and that he was to be ready to give covering fire with the men around him - He thoroughly understood the position and the tactics to be employed.

At this time, (about 9.00am) enemy apparently did not know where his own line was as he was shelling positions held by his troops.

I then returned to my Bn HQ at N.29.d.8.9 and carried on as per report already sent."

The attack proved to be one of the toughest which the battalion had encountered. The German resistance proved to be very strong ; Cerisy was honeycombed with isolated enemy machine-guns in concrete shelters and their fire proved deadly. The final result of a very arduous day's fighting being a slight gain of some 200-300 yards at the cost of appalling losses. The battalion was then withdrawn into reserve and positions occupied to provide against possible German counter-attacks.

A letter dated 24th April:

> "My dear Hu,
>
> We are still in the battle area, we came out of a fight last night, sad losses. The Battalion behaved most gallantly.
>
> Willy[13], Meggie[10] and Hookie[9] gone, all died fighting. Gibbo[14] and self are allright. Will write fuller later when I have time. We must be brave and carry on.
>
> Ever your old friend."

At the close of the actions between the 23rd and 27th April the 16th numbered less than 100 in all ranks. On the 27th the battalion marched to Arras, entrained for St Pol and marched to billets in Croissettes where they remained until 21st May.

It was whilst here that Elstob wrote to Captain Nash[7] who had been invalided home.

> "Dear Beau,
>
> I have been wanting to write to you ever since we came out of the fight. Tonight Major Roberts[15] has shewn me your letter in which you refer to our sad losses; to lose Megson[10], Wilson[13], Hook[9], Ingram[16] and Rylands[17] in one show is very very hard and they were all such gallant fellows.
>
> B Company, Beau, did very well indeed. MacDonnell[18] and J A Smith[19] were wounded and I have heard from the former. We were held up by machine guns and rifle fire; B Company were scattered about in shell holes all day, I was able to get to some of them but movement was difficult. Sergeant Leech[8] has been awarded the DCM for gallant conduct before the battle. Cpl Coxon[20], Cpl Profitt[21], and Sgt Gleave[22] have all been recommended for honours - they fought magnificently. I want you to know this, Beau, for I consider that it is due to your efforts and hard work that the Company proved itself so efficient.
>
> H R W Smith[23] was also wounded. I am sorry that you were not able to lead your Company into action.
>
> Meggy, Willy, Hook, how can we speak or write of them. I felt them all to be my friends and now they've gone.
>
> Of all the original officers of the Battalion I am now alone with Knowles[24], and I sometimes feel it almost a sin to be alive.
>
> We were able to bury all the officers in a neat little cemetery and yesterday afternoon we held a memorial service for the gallant dead in the warm spring sunshine under some budding lime trees in a quiet French village away from the firing line. It was not a cheerful ceremony but one was proud to be able to hold sacred communion with our Friends and Comrades. The end is not yet.
>
> Good-bye, Beau, this is going to be the year. With best wishes, Yours very sincerely."

A letter to Hubert Worthington dated 6th May 1917

"We are now resting and reorganising, but only for a short while, and we shall soon be moved on, I expect. Shea[25] and Weber[26] have both left us, the reason I don't exactly know. There are all sorts of rumours, I strongly suspect that the former left in loyalty to the latter. I was very fond of Weber, he was a charming man to meet. I have met both the new men in place of the above - a strict disciplinarian No 1 and another charming fellow No 2.

Hu, I hardly dare mention the losses, for my heart is full and I know how you will feel. On the battlefield as one moved about amongst shells and bullets - Death seemed a very small thing and at times enviable. Here we are English and German - we, or rather those dammed Journalists talk about Hate - it seems to me to disappear on the battlefield. People who have not been there talk a lot of dammed nonsense. We are all 'blind' ,as a private soldier on the night after the battle said to me - "We know it is not their quarrel sir" - this spontaneously.

Our fellows, it is always cigarettes or hot tea or something like that when they take prisoners and the Germans fed and kept alive our fellows in the midst of the bitterest Trones Wood fighting last year. Thank God. Humanity and unselfishness are higher than a lot of talked nonsense by certain petty-minded people.

The Vice-Admiral of Dover sends a wreath at the burial of German sailors killed in a fight in the Channel - why have we small minded people who object? God! I have seen German graves erected to the memory of our men and our graves erected to Germans - all in the most reverent manner. Thank God most of us who have fought and suffered and lost don't suffer from this pettiness - at least that is the way it strikes me.

Hubert, we have lost Meggie, Willy and Hookie whom you knew - Sergeants Ashton[27] and Dawson[28] & poor little Jimmy Mayors[29], L/Cpl Gibson[30] with you at Montauban and Pte Ogden[31] of "A" Company. Sergeant Ashton is missing and Clegg[31] (both believed killed). I haven't written to their next of kin yet in the case of the last two for there is a shadow of uncertainty.

Knowles[24] (Transport Officer) and myself are the last of the two very originals out here. I should be miserable if I were taken away from the battalion. I want to be with them in the battles, and if I were taken away on the battlefield I feel that I could die happily."

(Hubert Worthington kept a notebook in which he had details of all of his men ... their civilian occupations, next of kin etc. He describes Ashton as ' a good fellow - Good and keen shot....always an exemplary private in "A" Company. Anxious to be made L/Cpl. In an early entry Mayors is described as 'sloppy and unmilitary but not a bad fellow'. A later entry describes him as 'Excellent - coolest on earth'.)

A letter dated 10th May 1917

> "The Army commander came round to inspect us two days ago and I think that he was pleased with what he saw: today we had the Corps Commander inspecting our field operation and on Saturday we have to do a ceremonial parade before the Corps Commander, who I believe is Tom's[33] old divisional General. No time for more now, send us out some keen good officers, they are more than necessary."

The next few weeks continued in much the same way, a mixture of trench warfare, much marching and close-quarter fighting. Leaving Croisettes on 21st May the battalion marched to La Kreule, two miles north of Hazebrouk. On the 25th, after five days marching, Colonel Elstob wrote,

> "We have been marching a great deal lately, and I am glad to say that the battalion has marched very well. For two days never a man fell out. It has been a triumph in this hot weather, and I am proud of the men."

A letter dated 8th July 1917.

> "Since my return from leave we have had a nasty difficult time. For seven days we were in the worst trench sector that I have known out here and we had just over fifty casualties! The officers that come out now are very different to the old crowd, although many of them are excellent fellows - I find it difficult to get to know them and at times I feel terribly lonely and that my work is not as good as it was. Well anyway we shall be getting a chance of showing everybody what we can do. Sometimes Hubert my heart aches for a Friend to go and unburden myself to.
>
> Balleine[34] is leaving us. We are very busy, but are resting behind the lines - you will understand it all. If ever anything happens to me out here , quietly "Be Glad" Hubert, for it is with the 16th that I would lay down my life."

The general attack against the Flanders Ridge in the Ypres area was launched at dawn on 31st July 1917. For three successive days before the attack extra reconnaissance was made by the battalion to determine the forward assembly points for the attack and to remove obstacles and wire. On the night of 27/28th July Elstob himself led a large patrol, consisting of all his company commanders and representatives of each section of the battalion, and they penetrated to the forward German support trenches, gaining invaluable information about the ground which they were going to have to cross.

Zero hour on the 31st was at 0350 and began with one of the most concentrated artillery barrages of the war. The battalion gained all their objectives well into the first hour and at 0500, as no reports were coming in, Elstob went forward himself to assess the situation. Reaching a bend on the Ypres - Menin Road he found considerable confusion owing to different units being mixed up and at the same time under enemy machine gun and sniper fire. Showing again his absolute fearlessness and powers of leadership he gathered the men together and, moving them in small parties, proceeded to mop up the local enemy resistance. He returned to his own HQ at 1030 having obtained a good knowledge of the immediate local situation.

A letter dated 10th August 1917

"My Dear Hubert, We have just come from another "Show" and they tell me that the Battalion has done very well, but I sometimes feel very sick at heart, for dear Arthur Deaville[35], an A Coy original and one of the clerks in the Orderly Room has now gone - he was killed by a bursting shell about 3,500 yards behind our front line. I was very fond of him, and the poor fellow only became engaged on his last leave about six weeks ago. Deaville was a great friend of Canon Peter Green. My servant was badly hit, the H'dqrs Mess Cook Lance Corporal Wycherley[36] was killed. The Adjutant's servant wounded, all by the same shell.

I lost a topping youngster who commanded B Coy Captain Brodrick[37], he was so keen and tried so very hard. Many another gallant fellow has not come back.

Let us peg along, get the dammed show over as quickly and speedily as possible. I am very sorry to say that our new Padre was wounded in the recent operations, so that we have lost him. Ball[38], Knowles, Gibbon and Roberts are still with us."

A letter dated 26th August 1917

"I don't suppose you ever knew Gibbon's servant Walker[39], he was one of the originals, enlisted in the 17th at the age of forty-five, he died from wounds from the same shell that caused Deauville's death - he and Arthur Deauville were great friends, and I am proud to feel that they were both mine too. Poor Deauville got engaged on his last leave about eight weeks ago. I have not got his fiancee's address, but probably I shall do so when I hear from his people; he volunteered to come into the last action, he did not wish to be left behind.

At present I am acting as Brigadier, our present General being on leave; it is rather interesting and amusing being at Brigade Headquarters, the officers are a jolly good set of fellows, and our new Brigade Major is a splendid youngster.

I know that you will be very glad to hear that Macdonald[40] who has commanded our 19th Battn for some time has been awarded the Bar to his DSO, there is, I am sure nobody in the Division who more thoroughly deserves it, we are all very pleased.

I hope to come on leave sometime next month or at the beginning of October - do try and get some time off."

During the period between August and December 1917 Elstob temporarily commanded the 90th Brigade.

A letter dated 20th December 1917

"Just a hurried line my dear friend for this Xmas and that fateful year of 1918. We are in rather a lively sector at the present time, and the Hun attacked one of our battalions the other night, we were in the front line on their immediate right, but beyond securing three Hun prisoners we saw very little of the show. The men of this battalion were splendid, and I feel confident that if Master Boche had tried any of his little tricks that he would have had a very rough journey.

We have got a really splendid set of young officers from the cadet school in England, they are keen and have all seen considerable service out here. the Brigadier was very pleased with the way that the battalion did. I know Hu that you will be delighted to hear that old "Tom" Arnfield[41] and little Walker[42] of No 4 Platoon - now both of them Sergeants have been awarded the Military Medal - we got four for our last tour in the line. We were ordered to stand to again today, but thank God nothing serious happened."

A letter dated 29th December 1917

"I am afraid that my correspondence has been rather sketchy, but throughout all this Xmas time we have been and still are holding a most important sector of trenches, but I believe that we may be relieved soon. I am again acting for the General who is away on leave. Yesterday afternoon the Battalion Hdqrs that I should normally have occupied was blown in and there were about six casualties, some miraculous escapes; one officer not of our battalion being killed. The C.O. acting for me was wounded, the whole thing was damnable business."

Christmas was spent in the line near Zonnebeke and was the first time that the 16th had been in the front line on Christmas Day.

1918

The New Year of 1918 found the battalion in a camp on the outskirts of Reninghelst where they stayed for some four or five days. In January Elstob was awarded the Distinguished Service Order for his bravery and leadership in the third battle of Ypres on 31st July 1917.

Elstob was on UK leave in early January when a draft of 13 officers and 280 OR's arrived from the 19th Battalion following its disbandment as the junior battalion of the brigade in accordance with army re-organisation.

A letter dated 10th January 1918

> "We are out of the line now Hubert, and do you know I am writing this letter only 300 yards away from that hospital to where you were brought after our great battle of July 1st. God knows as one walks down the streets of this town, one's mind is full of old recollections:
>
> I passed my old billet the other day which Allen[4], Oliver[43] and Dalgleish[44] shared with me, Oliver and Allen! Hu those were the days weren't they dear Boy. Tatty[45] was in the kitchen helping there. We are on our way forward and shall probably pass the spot where you used to sunbathe.
>
> I am hoping for leave within the next two months. God bless you dear Friend."

The Officers 16th Battalion. Wilfrith Elstob seated in the centre.
Photograph probably taken January 1918 in the area of Reninghelst, Nr Poperinghe during training and re-organisation.

In February he captained a divisional football team against a French eleven in Paris. Not many Commanding Officers were fit enough or had the enthusiasm to enter into such activity.

MANCHESTER HILL

On the evening of 18th March 1918 the 90th Brigade took over the left sector of the line held by 30th Division in the centre of the front opposite St Quentin. The positions occupied by the Brigade were typical of the Fifth Army defences - organised in depth and planned to effect the utmost economy in men, whilst employing to best advantage the fire power of rifle, mortar, Lewis machine gun and Vickers machine gun.

Elstob spoke to the battalion before they moved into their sector and fully explained the proposed system of defence. It was known that a great attack was imminent and that they were one of the battalions which would bear the brunt of the attack. He warned his men that they had to be ready for a bombardment which might last several days and that they must hold up the enemy advance and not cause other troops to be sacrificed in regaining a lost position. *'It must be impressed upon all troops......that there is only one degree of resistance, and that is to the last round and to the last man'*. Pointing to the blackboard showing the company locations he said *'This is Battalion HQ. Here we fight and here we die'*.

Later as they marched up to the line a platoon singing competition was held which was judged by the Divisional Commander. When the band turned back, for they were not to go into action, Elstob was heard to say *'Those are the only fellows that will come out alive'*.

16th Manchesters manned the 'forward zone' with 'A' and 'B' Companies, on the right and left respectively holding the "line of observation" and the "line of resistance'. The 'line of observation' was the extent of the British front line and consisted of a chain of sentry groups, the eyes of the battalion. These men had strict orders to withdraw when a hostile infantry attack was launched. The 'line of resistance', some 2,000 yards in length, consisted of a series of strong posts established chequer-wise along the general line. Two six-inch mortars and several Vickers machine guns were distributed amongst these posts which would have to bear the first shock of the enemy's assault.

The battalion was based on and around a small feature which had been known as Manchester Hill since its capture in 1917 by the 2nd Manchesters. It lies between the villages of Francilly Selency and Savy, controlling the important St Quentin - Savy road and had an admirable field of fire in every direction. To the east, and to the battalion's immediate front, the road dips into St Quentin and here the Germans had made a tremendous concentration of guns to support their coming grand attack. Safe in the hollow the vast German army waited because the British artillery had been instructed not to shell this large and important town too heavily.

Two platoons of C Company were in support on the right and their other two platoons on the left. Battalion HQ plus D Company occupied the Manchester Hill Redoubt with Headquarters located in the 'Brown Quarry' on the reverse slope. This provided excellent cover and location for dug-outs. Stokes mortars were in place on the crest of the Quarry and artillery fire was to be controlled from an observation post on the summit of the hill.

It was hoped that the battalion would have time to get accustomed to the ground before the attack began.. The first night passed quietly as did the following two days. The night of 20th/21st March was calm and still. The sky was clear, the moon almost at full. A careful system of patrols covered the front throughout the night, but no enemy activity was reported. Elstob visited all the posts of the right half of the battalion whilst another officer from Battalion HQ visited the left half. At 5.30 am the final patrol went out. Time wore on. No news was sent in and the silence was complete.

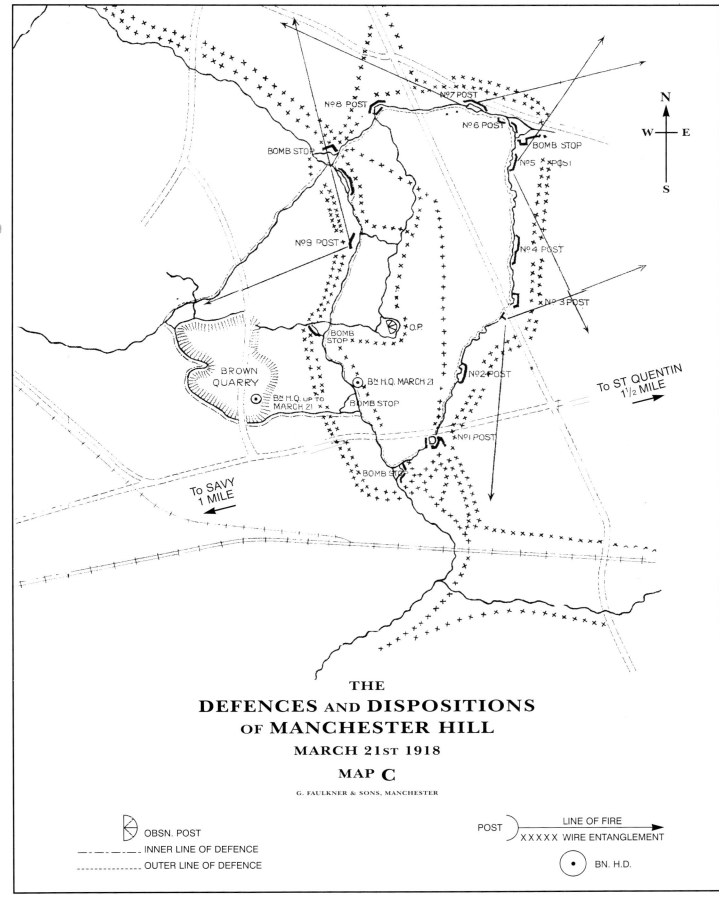

At 6.30 am the roar of innumerable heavy guns broke the calm. High explosives, shrapnel and, worst of all, gas shells shrieked through the air. The sky was lit up with great flashes; the much anticipated bombardment had begun. But still no enemy movement could be seen as fog had succeeded the clear and calm night - a fog made increasingly dense by the smoke of the bursting shells. Nothing could have been more disastrous. the wide front, the defence in depth, the valleys no longer death traps, gave the enemy everything he could desire.

At 7.30 am the companies in the front line reported that everything appeared normal and that the enemy shells were falling behind their positions. Elstob gave orders for Battalion HQ to move from the Brown Quarry to their Battle Headquarters on Manchester Hill. He then visited all the posts in the Redoubt, giving words of encouragement and telling the men what to do. Shortly after 8 am the bombardment became more intense and the telephone wires to the companies failed, although a buried cable ensured continued communication with Brigade HQ.

At about 8.30 am the first news of the beginning of the attack reached Battalion HQ when a runner arrived with the information that A Company Headquarters was almost surrounded. Within a few minutes similar news came from B Company. The thick fog made observation impossible and completely neutralised the elaborate scheme of machine gun defence which should have proved an impenetrable barrier to the enemy. At about 9 am a forward post on the left front of Manchester Hill sent back word that they were engaged at close quarters with the enemy, simultaneously the attack developed on the right post and from then on the desperate struggle raged on until late in the afternoon.

Gradually the fog lifted and by 11.30 there was a glint of sunshine breaking through. On all sides of Manchester Hill the enemy could be seen advancing by half-companies in file towards Savy. The break-through was complete on either side and special troops were left to settle with Manchester Hill. Completely surrounded the small garrison fought against overwhelming odds. Apart from the men of D Company many of them were not really used to fighting - cooks, signallers, batmen and regimental police - all the 'odd - job' collection that makes up an Infantry Battalion Headquarters - but they rose to the occasion, inspired by the supreme example of their Commander.

When the enemy entered the Redoubt by a trench leading from the Savy - St Quentin road Elstob erected a bombing block between the attackers and the Headquarters dug-out. Sniped at and bombed by the enemy he replied by emptying his revolver on a German bombing party a few yards down the trench, accounting for all of them. When his revolver ammunition was exhausted he continued to hold single-handed with bombs the post which he had already sustained against some half-dozen bombing attacks.

The enemy subsequently changed tactics and after a sharp bombardment made an attack in large numbers over the top. Elstob then took up a rifle and played a major part in holding them back. Only a few reached the parapet of the trench, into which they threw their bombs. Elstob was wounded here for the first time, but after his wound was dressed he returned to the defence, walking about regardless of the enemy fire from all sides, and cheering his men wherever he went. *'You are doing magnificently, boys! Carry on - keep up a steady fire and they'll think there's a battalion here'.*

According to Sergeant Arrundale[46], the Battalion Signals Sergeant: "In the afternoon the Colonel took up a rifle and twice crossed the Quarry, the entrance to which was already occupied by the enemy, to cheer up and encourage the Lewis Gunners. I saw him blown five yards by a 77mm shell which had dropped by his side. He was wounded three times but said to me

'Arrundale, they can't damn well kill me'. He asked brigade for a reinforcement of 20 men in order to make a counter-attack but this could not be done". By 2 pm most of the men on Manchester Hill were either dead or wounded and the final hand to hand fighting was taking place.

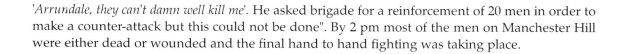

The Manchester Regiment will hold Manchester Hill to the last man. The romance of that amazing conversation on the buried cable between the Colonel and the Brigadier will never die. At the time a Staff Officer at Brigade Headquarters reported the episode as follows:

"At about 11 o'clock Colonel Elstob informed me that the Germans had broken through and were swarming round the Redoubt. At about 2 pm he said that most of his men were killed or wounded, including himself; that they were all getting dead-beat, that the Germans had got into the Redoubt and hand-to-hand fighting was going on. He was still quite cheery. At 3.30 he was spoken to on the telephone and said that very few were left and that the end was nearly come. After that no answer could be got".

At about 3 pm a German plane came overhead and at the same time German field artillery pieces were brought up to within 60 yards of the Redoubt. Within the next half hour few of the defenders remained alive. One survivor told of the last words that Elstob used to him were *'Tell the men not to lose heart. Fight on!'*. He still held his ground, firing from some twenty-five to thirty yards up the trench. A last assault was made by the enemy who called on Elstob to surrender. He replied "*Never*" and was shot dead. By 4 pm it was all over and the battered remnants of the 16th, wounded and exhausted, surrendered.

EPILOGUE

The following month, on 15th April 1918, an impressive tribute to Wilfrith Elstob and the men of the 16th Manchesters was paid at a memorial service in Manchester Cathedral. Those present included his Father Canon Elstob, the Lord Mayor and members of the City Corporation. Wounded soldiers were present in large numbers. Bishop Weldon gave the address in which he said they would forever recall the splendid gallantry of The Manchesters.

Manchester Cathedral.

FORM OF SERVICE

TO BE HELD

IN MEMORY OF THE

OFFICERS, NON-COMMISSIONED OFFICERS AND MEN

Of the Manchester Regiment who laid down their lives in defence of the Manchester Hill Redoubt, near St. Quentin, in France, at Passion Tide, 1918.

APRIL 15th, 1918.

Of the 8 officers and 160 other ranks who went into action on Manchester Hill only 2 officers and 15 other ranks survived. These, together with the survivors from the rifle companies moved on 16th May to Monthieres and were attached to the American 1st Battalion 140th Regiment to assist in its training. From 11th June to the 15th they were with the 3rd Battalion 138th Regiment US Army. The cadre of the battalion returned to England for a two week period resting and receiving drafts of officers and men Then back to France where the 16th continued fighting until 31st October 1918. The Armistice was declared on 11th November.

At the end of the war Hubert Worthington journeyed to St Quentin to find his friend's body, but without success. The War Graves Commission had been unable to identify him. In May 1919 Worthington went once again to France to meet a party from the Commission with the purpose of digging on the Redoubt under his supervision. Sadly no identifiable body cold be found.

However later that year Hubert Worthington was responsible for ensuring that 'Bindy' received due acknowledgement for his bravery; personally collating statements from the survivors and submitting the successful case for the award of the Victoria Cross. It was entirely due to the efforts of his greatest friend that Wilfrith Elstob's name and the memory of all those who fought and fell with him were not forgotten.

In the June 1919 edition of The Blue - the journal of Christ's Hospital - one who knew him well, both at Merchiston and in France, wrote: "He was one of the finest men in the Division; a man of unusually strong personality. Everyone who came in touch with him felt the force of it, from Divisional Commander to Private soldier. I happened to hear from two successive Divisional Commanders what a particularly fine fellow they thought him and I know his own officers and men worshipped him. He was one of the most modest men I have ever known. Whether commanding a brigade, as he did for a time last year, or a platoon as he did barely two years ago, he was just the same. He got an MC of course and then a DSO. He was the kind of man to whom such things are bound to come, but they did not affect him one way or another. His extremely high sense of duty was an inspiration to all who knew him well. Generous, unassuming, fearless, cool in action, absolutely dependable - these are the qualities that seem to me to stand out above others. Perhaps, after all, he was 'big'.

1919

A choral celebration of the Holy Communion was held at Christs Hospital on 20th July 1919 in memory of all brothers fallen in the war. These included Wilfrith Elstob and 2nd Lieutenant Edward Felix Baxter of The King's (Liverpool) Regiment who had also been awarded the Victoria Cross.

On 24th July 1919 John Elstob, accompanied by Hubert Worthington went to Buckingham Palace where HM King George V presented him with the Victoria Cross awarded to his son.

> Fairlawn,
> Chelford,
> Cheshire.
> July 22.
>
> Dear Hubert,
>
> I go to London on Thursday, & stay at the Berners Hotel till Saturday.
>
> The Investiture is at 10.30. Two tickets have been enclosed for relatives or friends to witness the Ceremony, so I do most earnestly hope that you – his greatest friend – will be there.
>
> What a help it would be to know that you are by my side! Alas! Eric cannot be – as he yesterday went to Droitwich. The dear lad does not somehow get rid of that sciatica.
>
> On Sunday I wrote to J. Watt asking if he could take me in for the week-end, how sweet if we could be there together.
>
> Bunny is now, I hope, nearing England. He reached Batoum on June 26th & was then waiting for a boat. His journey will be by sea, as the overland route is closed.
>
> Your affectionate
> J. G. Elstob

Letter from John George Elstob to Hubert Worthington.

Capesthorne Vicarage,
Chelford,
Cheshire.
Ap: 11. 18.

Dear Mr Barrington,
You loving letter has deeply affected me, & I shall always treasure it.

Rudge — your Colonel's orderly — escaped after being taken a prisoner at the Redoubt, & he reported at Brigade Head Quarters that he saw his wounded Colonel & Major Gibbon both taken prisoners. So there is ground for hope in believing that some, at any rate, of the heroes of Manchester Hill are prisoners.

I have had no further information, but enclose 2 cuttings, one from the "Daily News" & the other from "The Daily Despatch."

I possess only one large photograph of my son, but I believe that copies of it are about to be taken in Manchester, & when they are ready I will send you one.

Believe me
Always Sincerely Yours
J. G. Elliot
F—the of you beloved Colonel.

Letter to Harold Barrington, ex-16th Battalion.

MANCHESTER REGT.

LT. COL. W. ELSTOB. V.C.
LT. COL. C. S. WORTHINGTON
MJR. J. R. HOUGHTON
MJR. A. J. MOORHOUSE
MJR. J. E. ROWBOTHAM
CPT. L. B. BAIRD
CPT. R. H. BEDFORD
CPT. R. BENTHAM
CPT. P. A. BLYTHE
CPT. R. L. BOLTON
CPT. E. BRODRICK

TO THE MEMBERS OF THE UNIVERSITY of MANCHESTER AND OF THE OFFICERS TRAINING CORPS WHO LAID DOWN THEIR LIVES IN THE :: GREAT WAR 1914-1919 ::
IN GRATEFUL ::
AND ENDURING
REMEMBRANCE

HE HAS BOUGHT HIS ETERNITY WITH A LITTLE HOUR AND IS NOT DEAD

Manchester University war memorial.

1923

On 31st January 1923 a simple ceremony was held at the Toc H Headquarters in 'Victoria Park, Manchester when Canon Elstob dedicated a small library as the Wilfrith Elstob and 16th Manchesters Room. Over the fireplace hung a photograph of the gallant Colonel. In the 1980s this building was no longer in use and the framed photograph and various brass memorial plaques were transferred to the Headquarters of The Manchesters Company of the 5th/8th Battalion The King's Regiment at Ardwick Green in Manchester where they are permanently displayed.

The commemorative plaque and (on facing page) the Elstob memorial window in Siddington Church.

Wilfrith's father - John George Elstob - was the much loved Vicar of Siddington from 1888 until his retirement in 1927. He had been appointed Rural Dean of Macclesfield in 1904 and made an Honary Canon of Chester Cathedral in 1911. He died in October 1926 and is buried, with other members of his family, in the churchyard at Siddington.

1993

Sunday 21st March 1993, the 75th anniversary of the battle of Manchester Hill and the date when a very special ceremony was held at St James' Palace in London. The Victoria Cross and the medals awarded to Wilfrith Elstob are the property of his old school Christ's Hospital. It had however been agreed with the school that the most suitable and secure place for his medals to be displayed was with his old regiment in the Museum of The Manchesters in Ashton under Lyne.

1st Battalion The King's Regiment, the successor Regular Army battalion to the amalgamated King's Liverpool Regiment and The Manchester Regiment were then, in 1993, on London duties, providing ceremonial guards at Buckingham Palace, St James' Palace and the Tower of London. Pupils and staff from Christ's Hospital together with serving and retired officers of the Regiment were present in the Officers Mess of St. James Palace when the medals were handed over to the Regiment for safe keeping.

The Chapel of The Manchester Regiment and The King's Regiment in Manchester Cathedral contains a shrine in which the memorial books with the names of the men who died are displayed. Wilfrith Elstob and his comrades of the 16th Battalion are there and a separate shrine contains a book devoted to the citations of those who have been awarded the Victoria Cross and the George Cross. The pages of these memorial books are turned every fortnight at a short service held by members of the Regimental Association.

Memorial to the 16th, 17th, 18th & 19th Manchester Pals in Montauban.

1996

On 30th June 1996 a memorial was erected by The King's Regiment in the village of Francilly Selency. It occupies a special position on the lawn between the Mairie and the church, adjacent to the French memorial to the men of the village who lost their lives in the war of 1914/18 and the memorial to those who fell in the battle of St Quentin on 18th/19th January 1871 during the Franco/Prussian war.

The regimental memorial is for Manchester Hill, which is just a short distance from the village, and to the men of the 2nd Manchesters who originally established its name and to Wilfrith Elstob with his men of the 16th Manchesters. They made its name as famous in the proud history of the British Army as did their predecessors in the Regiment at the battles of Bunker Hill and Inkerman.

Memorial to the 2nd and 16th Battalions in Francilly Selency.

Representing the Regiment at the unveiling of the Francilly Selency memorial were Kingsmen from 1st Battalion The King's Regiment (then stationed in Cyprus) and C (The Manchesters) Company 5th/8th (Volunteer) Battalion The King's Regiment, together with members of The King's and Manchester Regiment Association.

*The Ryleys School, Alderley Edge, Cheshire where one of the four school houses is named Elstob.
His name and brief details are inscribed on a wall in the school dining hall.*

Pozieres British Cemetery.

*The names of Wilfrith Elstob. Claude Worthington[1], Edward Brodrick[37] and their comrades who died but whose
bodies were never recovered are inscribed on panels 64 to 67 of the memorial wall which encloses
Pozieres British Cemetery, six miles north-west of Arras.*

A stained glass window to his memory is to be found in his father's lovely old church at Siddington in Cheshire. His name is on the memorial board in the Memorial Hall at Merchiston Castle School, Edinburgh, on the war memorial at Manchester University and at the Ryleys School, Alderley Edge in Cheshire.

On 1st July 1958 two large candlesticks of English Oak were dedicated in the Regimental Chapel. One was presented by the Old Comrades Association of the 16th Battalion in memory of their Colonel. His name is inscribed on the base with a carving of the Victoria Cross.

INDEX

(1) Hubert Worthington and Wilfrith Elstob had been close friends since their days together as young boys at the Ryleys School in Alderley Edge. Worthington spent almost a year in hospital recovering from his wounds. He was then posted as an instructor of officer cadets at Crookham Camp - Salisbury Plain. He never returned to the 16th. Later to become a distinguished architect and knighted. He was one of the founders of the Manchester Regiment Chapel in Manchester Cathedral and was responsible for its restoration after its destruction during WW2. The window of flames at the east end of the Regimental Chapel is the Regiment's memorial to him.

(2) Captain F Walker DCM. A pre-war soldier who had acted as Quartermaster in the early days of the battalion at Heaton Park but had taken command of B Company by the time they went to France.

(3) Captain William Morton Johnson MA, FRGS. Age 34. Killed in action 2nd July 1916 at Montauban. In civilian life he had been the Chairman and Managing Director of the Manchester engineering firm Richard Johnson, Clapham & Morris. Name on the Thiepval memorial.

(4) Lieutenant Sidney Raymond Allen. Killed in action 12th July 1916 at Montauban. Name on the Thiepval memorial.

(5) Lieutenant Arnold Kerry (ex Devonshire Regiment). Buried Cambridge City Cemetery, UK.

(6) Lieutenant Colonel Hubert Knox. Killed in action 13th October 1916 A Regular Army officer of 2nd Manchesters who had been severely wounded at the battle of Le Cateau. He became Second in Command of the 16th and assumed command on 10th July following the battle at Trones Wood. Buried in Caterpillar Valley Cemetery, France. Plot VIII B2.

(7) Captain Anthony Havelock Nash. Following active service with the Gloucestershire Regiment he was commissioned into The Manchester Regiment and joined the 16th Battalion on 13th May 1915 at Heaton Park as the junior subaltern officer. Following Montauban he was given command of B Company which he continued to command until 1st April 1917 when he was invalided to the UK

(8) Sergeant R Leech DCM. (43008)

(9) Lieutenant Cyril Walter Keenan Hook. Killed in action 23rd April 1917. Age 21. Buried Wancourt British Cemetery. Plot V E 9. In civilian life he had worked for the Manchester engineering firm Mather & Platt.

(10) Captain Robert Hargraves Megson. Killed in action 23rd April 1917. Age 29. Twice mentioned in despatches. Name on the Arras Memorial.

(11) Lieutenant Colonel Claude Swanwick Worthington DSO & bar, TD. Also a pupil at the Ryleys Preparatory School. A graduate of Manchester University and brother of Hubert Worthington. A pre-war Territorial officer, he commanded the 6th Battalion The Manchester Regiment. Died of wounds, on 14th October 1918. Buried Mont Huon Military Cemetery. Name on the War Memorial at Manchester University and inscribed in the dining room of the Ryleys School.

(12) Lieutenant Colonel Maurice Edwin McConaghey DSO. Royal Scots Fusiliers. Killed in action on 23rd April 1917.

(13) Captain Lawrence Farrer Wilson. Killed in action on 23rd April 1917. Age 29. Name on the Arras Memorial In civilian life he had worked for the Manchester firm Fred Taylor & Sons.

(14) Major Robert Gibbon (Awarded Military Cross 1/1/1918) He went to France with the 16th in 1915, remaining with it throughout. Appointed Adjutant 10th July 1916. At Manchester Hill he helped to stop many of the enemy rushes during the morning until severely wounded in the right arm and shoulder by a "pineapple" bomb. Taken prisoner.

(15) Major Rupert Edward Roberts. Died of wounds on 26th March 1918 received at Moyencourt. Buried St Seven Cemetery, Rouen, France. Plot B 5. 11. After Manchester Hill he collected as many of the 16th together - in all two subalterns and seventy men - to fight a bitter and unequal rear guard action. The battalion was reinforced to a strength of 450 on 27th / 28th March.

(16) 2nd Lieutenant John A Ingram. Killed in action 23rd April 1917.

(17) 2nd Lieutenant Frank Rylands. Killed in action 23rd April 1917.

(18) 2nd Lieutenant R A M J MacDonnel. Wounded 23rd April 1917.

(19) 2nd Lieutenant J A Smith. Wounded 23rd April 1917.

(20) Corporal H Coxon (17324)

(21) Corporal A Proffitt MM (6545)

(22) Sergeant W Gleave MM.(7374)

(23) 2nd Lieutenant H R W Smith. Wounded 23rd April 1917.

(24) Captain R K Knowles. He held the proud distinction of having gone right through the war with the 16th. Joining in September 1914 he went to France in November 1915 in command of 11 Platoon, C Company. In April 1916 he beame Transport Officer which duties, according to one of his brother officers, he fulfilled with conspicuous ability and courage until March 1918. During the whole of that time supplies never failed to reach the troops no matter what action they were in or what their position was. He took over command of B Company after Manchester Hill. His company behaved with great gallantry during the German attack near Hollebeke in May 1918.

(25) Major General Sir John Shea GCN KCMG DSO. Commander 30th Division. Originally commissioned in the Royal Irish Rifles, later transferred into the Indian Army

(26) Colonel William Weber DSO. Chief of Divisional Staff. Commissioned in the Royal Artillery

(27) Sergeant Charles Edward Ashton (7074) Killed in action 23rd April 1917. Name on the Arras Memorial.

(28) Sergeant Herbert Dawson (6232) Killed in action 23rd April 1917. Age 26. Name on the Arras Memorial.

(29) Private James Mayors (6403) Killed in action 23rd April 1917. Name on the Arras Memorial. In civilian life he had worked for the Manchester textile company Tootal Broadhurst & Lee.

(30) Lance Corporal Henry Gibson (7653) Killed in action 2rd April 1917. Name on the Arras memorial.

(31) Private Harry Ogden (27349) Killed in action 23rd April 1917. Age 25. Buried Wancourt Military Cemetery. Plot V E 14.

(32) Lance Corporal George Reginald Clegg (6227). Killed in action 23rd April 1917. Age 23. Name on the Arras memorial.

(33) Captain Thomas Worthington MC. 22nd Manchesters. Brother of Hubert and Claude Worthington. Very badly wounded on 1st July 1916 at Mametz.

(34) *The Reverend R W Balleine MC. He had been Padre to the battalion since its formation. (His medals are with the Museum of The Manchesters).*

(35) *Lance Corporal Arthur Deauville MM (6235) Killed in action 30th July 1917. Buried Lijssenthoek Military Cemetery, Belgium. Plot XVII E 14A.*

(36) *Lance Corporal Harry Wycherley (7071) Killed in action 3oth July 1917. Buried Railway Cutting Cemetery, Belgium.*

(37) *Captain Edward Brodrick. Killed in action 30th July 1917. A fellow graduate of Manchester University. Age 24. Name on the Menin Gate memorial, Ypres and on the war memorial at Manchester University.*

(38) *Lieutenant (QM) John Thomas Ball MC. Severely wounded on 21st March 1918.*

(39) *Private George Woodburn Walker (7293) Died of wounds on 7th August 1917. Age 47. Buried Wimereux Communal Cemetery. Plot H P 11.*

(40) *Lieutenant Colonel Charles Leslie Macdonald DSO (two bars). A pre-war Territorial officer. Had been Captain and Adjutant of the 17th Battalion from 10th June 1915. He commanded 19th Manchesters from March 1917 until its disbandment in February 1918*

(41) *Sergeant Tom Arnfield MM (6207). Hubert Worthington describes him as a Policeman in civilian life and conscientious.*

(42) *Sergeant Albert Walker MM (6642). Died of wounds on 8th April 1918. Age 22. Buried Mont Huon Cemetery. Plot VI G 25.*

(43) *Lieutenant John Milner Oliver. Killed in action on 9th July 1916 at Trones Wood. Age 34. Name on the Thiepval Memorial.*

(44) *Lieutenant A B Dalgleish. Invalided in April 1916 with jaundice and tuberculosis.*

(45) *Private Ernest Tattersall (6689). Killed in action on 1st July 1916. Buried Quarry Cemetery (Montauban). Plot 1V. F6.*

(46) *Sergeant S R Arrundale MM. Battalion Signals Sergeant.*

BIBLIOGRAPHY RELATING TO THE 16th MANCHESTERS

The Diary of an Unprofessional Soldier.
Edited by T A M Nash. 1991. ISBN 0 948251-48-4

Manchester Pals.
Michael Stedman. ISBN 0 85052 393 1. Pen and Sword Books, Barnsley 1994.

The 16th, 17th, 18th and 19th Battalions The Manchester Regiment. A Record 1914 - 1918.
Sherratt & Hughes, Manchester. 1923.

The Signal Section of the 16th Manchesters.
T E Pennington DCM. Privately published 1937.

Manchester City Battalions of the 90th & 91st Infantry Brigades - Roll of Honour.
Sherratt & Hughes 1916.
A photographic record, with names, of each platoon of the 16th to 23rd Pals Battalions., plus the names of the volunteers from companies and institutions in and around Manchester who were serving in the armed forces at that time.